A Picture

POST CARD

History of Fairhaven

Spinner Publication, Inc., New Bedford, Massachusetts
Printed in the United States of America
Support from the Massachusetts Cultural Council

Library of Congress Cataloging-in-Publication Data applied for

A Picture Postcard History of Fairhaven
text and design by Joseph D. Thomas and Jay Avila; cover by Mint Evans
120pp., 215 illus., 28 cm.

ISBN 0932027-75-X paper • 0932027-83-0 cloth

A Picture

History of Fairhaven

Postcards from the collections of

The Postcard Collaborators of Fairhaven

edited by

Joseph D. Thomas and Jay Avila

Spinner Publications, Inc.

New Bedford, Massachusetts

Foreword

Why collect picture postcards? Ask any collector and they will tell you that collecting is not just a hobby but a pleasant obsession. How many can you accumulate? What's the earliest and rarest card you can find on the subject?

In Fairhaven, Massachusetts, there are some very serious collectors. So many, in fact, that we decided to meet regularly at the Millicent Library to share our collections, talk about our discoveries, and trade postcards. In January 2002, we formed The Postcard Collaborators of Fairhaven.

Eventually, we determined that the best way to share our picture history was to publish a selection of our favorite postcards. It was decided that any profit derived from the sale of the book would become a donation to the Millicent Library Archives Fund. We invited the folks at Spinner Publications of New Bedford to come in and discuss how to get the project going, and voila! It was done.

The Collaborators hope you will have as much fun as we did reminiscing and learning about the fair town of Fairhaven.

— The Postcard Collaborators of Fairhaven

Acknowledgements

Our deepest thanks to the Millicent Library and its staff, particularly Debbie Charpentier, Archivist, for their assistance in producing this book.

Photographs were supplied by the Postcard Collaborators and their friends:

Millicent Allen   Max Isaksen
Robert Cormier   Sheila Tunstall McKenna
Arthur Frates   Cynthia McNaughton
Odette A. Furtado   Daniel A. Mello
Milton P. George   Marjorie Orman
Natalie S. Hemingway   Anthony Simmons, Jr.
Gail Isaksen   Jay S. Simmons

Design and typography by Joseph D. Thomas, Jay Avila and Mint Evans

Copy editors and Proofreaders:

Christopher Richard   Andrea V. Tavares
Jules Ryckebusch   Anne J. Thomas
Carolyn Longworth   Dianne Wood
Myra Lopes

Fairhaven, Mass. Old Fort Phoenix.

*Fairhaven is a Capital town. One is sure
of that, but the girls here keep you guessing
all the time.*

Contents

Henry H. Rogers

Henry Huttleson Rogers was born in Fairhaven on January 29, 1840. As a boy, he carried newspapers for the New Bedford **Evening Standard** and, after graduating from Fairhaven High School, worked as a baggage master at the railroad depot. At age 20, he headed for the oil fields of Pennsylvania, founded a refinery, and went on to become an executive with Pratt Refinery in Brooklyn. With continued success, he teamed up with John D. Rockerfeller to become executive vice president of Standard Oil Company of Ohio. At the time of his death in 1909, Rogers was worth over $100 million. He once told his dear friend Mark Twain, "My rule in business is to get the money in hand."

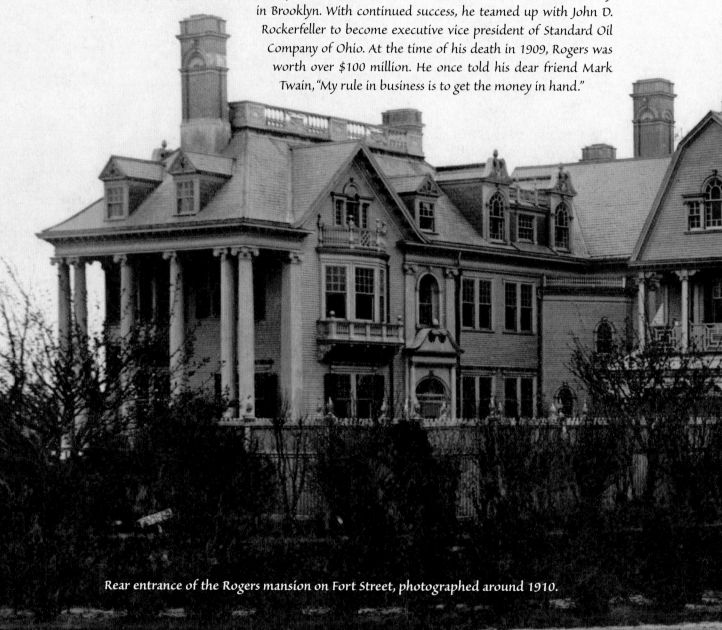

Rear entrance of the Rogers mansion on Fort Street, photographed around 1910.

ROGERS MANSION, FAIRHAVEN

Rogers served as president of six of the 20 companies formed after the government breakup of Standard Oil, and as vice president of 13. A shrewd and successful capitalist, he was also a generous philanthropist to his hometown of Fairhaven.

In addition to the beautiful buildings he gave to the town, Rogers financed Helen Keller's education, funded schools in the South for Booker T. Washington, sponsored Albert Bierstadt's art, paid off Mark Twain's debt, and gave generously to institutions such as St. Luke's Hospital and the Old Dartmouth Historical Society in New Bedford. He also built a grammar school in Mattapoisett and helped finance an Acushnet school.

This chapter features postcards of some of the projects created by Henry H. Rogers and his family.

ASS.

WOOD
34

A 21847 Residence of Mr. H. H Rogers, front View), Fairhaven, Mass.

The Rogers Mansion

Henry H. Rogers' 85-room mansion at the south end of Fort Street was built in 1895 as the family's summer home. It had 18 bedrooms, wide verandas, kitchens large enough for a deluxe hotel, a well-stocked wine cellar, bowling lanes, children's playrooms, stables, gardens, cold storage, and a gas plant. The home was built by architect Charles Brigham, who designed all but one of Rogers' Fairhaven buildings. This view shows the south side of the mansion, which faces Fort Phoenix. The front, or west side, to the left of the building, faces Fort Street.

Rogers' mansion overlooked New Bedford Harbor to the west and Buzzards Bay to the south. This view from the turret looks west toward Palmer's Island and the New Bedford shore.

WEST FROM ROGERS HOUSE FAIRHAVEN MASS   H.M. WOOD 58

In this view, the mansion's south lawn is transformed into a meadow of wild flowers.

In 1915, just six years after Rogers' death, his son Harry brought in the wrecking crew to tear down the mansion. Some sections of the estate were saved. The 37-room children's wing was purchased and moved to Doane Street. Auxiliary buildings such as the laundry house, the potting house, and the gardener's house were also sold and moved. Mayor James M. Curley of Boston purchased some of the interior woodwork. Others snapped up bargains such as a set of leaded glass windows for $15, chandeliers for $100, and mahogany doors for $15. Remnants of the interior, such as staircases, paneling, and fireplace mantels, can be found in houses throughout the area. This view shows the mansion's front side.

H. H. Rogers Residence Fairhaven Mass.

Unitarian Memorial Church

Built in 1903 and designed in 15th-century Perpendicular English Gothic style, The Unitarian Memorial Church with its attached sanctuary and separate English Tudor Manse (Parsonage), was a gift to Fairhaven in memory of Rogers' mother, Mary E. Rogers, who died in 1899. Architect Charles Brigham's design includes a 165-foot bell tower with a finely adjusted chime of 11 bells. Built from granite quarried from the ledge at Fort Phoenix, the church is listed in the National Register of Historic Places.

The Parish House is at left, the main sanctuary is at center, and the Parsonage is at right.

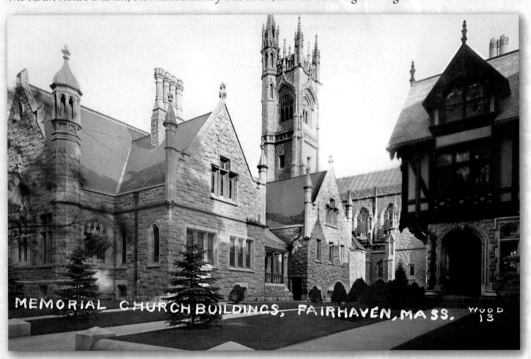

This interior view of the Unitarian Church looks toward a stained glass window created by Robert Reid of New York depicting the Nativity. Hand-carved oak fills the church interior—from pews to pulpit, from window casings to choir-screen. Even the four towering organ fronts are detailed with delicate carvings. The ceiling is supported by wood trusses capped with six-foot angels sporting wings tipped in gold leaf.

The auditorium of the Parish House rises to the full height of the edifice and is ornately paneled in hand-carved oak and Indian teak. Etched on the lower panes of the windows are poetry verses selected by New York poet-clergyman Robert Collyer. Decorative elements on the exterior include chimneys with ornate terra-cotta pots and corners capped with ogee-roofed lanterns.

Fairhaven High School

Fairhaven High School was built in 1906 and housed 67 rooms. Designed in the Elizabethan style by architect Charles Brigham, the high school was the last of six buildings that Rogers would bestow on the town. The foundation is of ashlar granite quarried from Fort Phoenix ledge.

At the intersection of Huttleston Avenue and Main Street, horses refuel at a statue-topped fountain erected by the Fairhaven Improvement Association. Drinking fountains were located at strategic points in town at a cost of $1200. "A fountain in a convenient locality for use of man and beast is not only desirable," wrote the Association, "but absolutely demanded as an act of humanity to the many horses that pass through the town."

New High School & Fountan Fairhaven Mass.

The High School from the Athletic Field, Fair Haven, Mass.   214658

From the east side of the high school can be seen the athletic field, in the foreground, and the unusual octagonal gymnasium wing attached to the rear of the building.

The athletic field, with its concrete grandstands, was built in the summer of 1907, and 15 high school students, ages 14–17, worked on the project. "I like to see the spirit of hard work and hustle that the boys of the High School have," said H. H. Rogers, who stopped by every day to watch the boys work. "We have a good time of it," said one of the boys," for we can go to work at 7:00 and have an hour-and-a-half for dinner, or we can start at 7:30 and have an hour for dinner, so you see, if we feel tired at night, we can sleep a half-hour extra in the morning. We are given a dollar a day and that is good pay for boys our size and age, but we do nearly as much work as the regular gang."

Stadium of Fairhaven High School,
Fairhaven, Mass.

This card shows the basement room where students learned woodworking and construction skills. When the building opened, the classroom was fully equipped and supplied, courtesy of Henry H. Rogers.

At the time of its construction, the high school gymnasium was the only octagonal gym in the world and was considered the most beautiful in the country. It was stocked by Rogers with state-of-the-art equipment. The backside of this postcard reads, "Here is where we have physical excercise. The girls have to wear bloomers and middy blouses. We play basket ball, hockey, indoor base ball and then we have all kinds of drills with dumb bell and indian clubs. This is the hall where the Seniors have their dances. The ropes are for the boys only."

In the laboratory kitchen, located in the school's basement, girls were taught culinary skills using the latest tools of the trade. Fairhaven High School was one of the first schools in the country to use natural gas.

The study room, or Room 7, is the school's largest, measuring 67 by 22 feet. Its Renaissance-style ceiling is adorned with cherubs and plaster medallions in bas relief. The light fixtures feature cherubs blowing trumpets. The permanently installed desks and chairs are made of quartered oak and seat more than 100 students.

Tabitha Inn

Located two blocks east of the Unitarian church, the Tabitha Inn is named for Rogers' great grandmother. One architecture critic called it "a well-planned and most attractive appearing country hotel," but noted: "Severe criticism would probably declare that the would-be antiquated sign-post before the entrance was a particularly unsuccessful attempt to reproduce an old-time feature..." (**New England Magazine**, June 1907)

Tabitha Inn, Fairhaven, Mass.

TABITHA INN, FAIRHAVEN, MASS. WOOD 8

The Tabitha Inn, pictured here around 1916, housed as many as 130 guests and was officially recommended by the Automobile Club of America. According to legend, the inn was built at the suggestion of Mark Twain, who pointed out that, because the beautiful memorial church would attract hundreds of sightseers, a place of comfort was needed to accommodate them. The Tudor-style inn, built in 1905, also hosted functions and social gatherings until 1942, when it was leased to the Coast Guard to board trainees. In 1944 it was purchased by the Fall River Diocese, and today is occupied by Our Lady's Haven nursing home.

Ladies in traditional whites slug it out on the inn's tennis court, circa 1910.

TABITHA INN, FAIRHAVEN, MASS.

Millicent Library

In August 1890, Millicent Gifford Rogers, the tycoon's daughter, died of a heart ailment at age 17. Crushed by the untimely passing of Millicent, whom he called "the dear girl whose memory we adore and desire to perpetuate," Rogers decided to erect a public library as a memorial gift from her brother and three sisters.

This interior view of the Library is from a set of postcards published in 1943. The Trustees' Room, with fireplace and ornate meeting table, has many beautiful works of art gracing its walls.

Trustées Room
THE MILLICENT LIBRARY
Fairhaven, Massachusetts

Mark Twain described it as "the ideal library." At right, Director Avis Pillsbury assists a patron at the circulation desk, circa 1943. Behind them, a 16-foot stained-glass memorial window, crafted in 1891 by Clayton & Bell of London, displays the likeness of William Shakespeare with Millicent Rogers as the muse of poetry.

Below is the Reading Room, 1943, with its oak tables, handsome reading lamps, and exotic statuettes. The library walls are trimmed with plaster-cast bas relief designs and beautifully carved English oak.

Reading Room
THE MILLICENT LIBRARY
Fairhaven, Massachusetts

Rogers School

The Rogers School was the first building given by Henry H. Rogers to Fairhaven. At its dedication in 1885, Rogers reflected that 30 years earlier the town had rejected efforts to build a new school. He felt that the vote was influenced by those with money who didn't want to spend it. He remembered being told, "The taxpayers would settle such matters without the assistance of shallow-padded boys."

The Rogers School was designed by architect Warren R. Briggs and dedicated on September 3, 1885. Students began classes four days later and still attend class there today.

ATLAS TACK WORKS, FAIRHAVEN, MASS.

In 1865, the American Nail Company of Boston moved into waterfront property on Fort Street and founded the Atlas Tack Company, the town's principal industry for 120 years. In 1891, Rogers acquired the struggling enterprise along with several other tack makers in the state, consolidating them into a modern factory on Pleasant Street. The new plant flourished, employing hundreds of local residents until its closing in 1985.

The George H. Taber Masonic Lodge, on Main and Centre streets, was the first Masonic Lodge to be named for a living person. Mr. Taber was the town's oldest Mason and Rogers' former Sunday School teacher. "His heart is as big as an ox," Rogers declared, "and he has love enough for all the world. He has been a father to me, a father to my mother, the most precious thing on earth." The building was designed as a business block with storefronts at street level and the lodge hall and rooms on the second and third floors.

Fairhaven Town Hall

The Town Hall was presented to Fairhaven on February 22, 1894, by Henry H. Rogers' wife Abbie, who died three months after its dedication. Fairhaven had been in desperate need of a building after fire destroyed the first town hall in 1858. Since then, town meetings had been held in various halls and churches. Mark Twain, who spoke at the dedication, praised Rogers for making such gifts while alive: "If you wait till you're dead there is barren result and a divided profit. You get the credit for the intention, and the lawyers get the money."

Young patriots demonstrate their colors on the Town Hall steps, circa 1915.

Town Hall, Fairhaven, Mass.

There is no ft. of Snow here.
A Merry Xmass and Happy New Year
Arthur

Designed by Charles Brigham in French Gothic style with ashlar granite and Delmonico brick, the Town Hall came equipped with heavy oak tables and armchairs, an 800-seat auditorium, and stained-glass windows. When the clock was installed in August 1893, the clock on the nearby Methodist Church had to be stopped because the simultaneous chiming caused confusion.

A view along William Street at the town center showing the Town Hall and the Millicent Library.

Cushman Park, dedicated in 1908, was the last of Rogers' gifts to Fairhaven. It was created by filling in the old Mill Pond—a remarkable feat at the time. The 13-acre pond—a tidal swamp eating away at prime land along Bridge and Spring Streets—was a nuisance to developers and a threat to the new high school. It also blocked road access from the town center to Oxford Village. To fill the pond, which was as deep as 25 feet in places, Rogers had a small-gauge railroad built to transport soil from Bridge Street near Alden Road to the pond. The project took six years and cost around $70,000 to complete. The park is named for Robert Cushman, Rogers' Puritan ancestor.

On Huttleston Avenue and Main Street, in front of Fairhaven High School, the Henry H. Rogers Memorial stands in tribute to the man who gave so much to his native town. The monument was designed by architect Charles Brigham and dedicated on January 29, 1912, the 72nd anniversary of Mr. Rogers' birth. The tablet on the Memorial reads (from Latin): "If you want to see his work, look about you."

2184 - Memorial to H. H. Rogers, Fairhaven, Mass.

The Rogers family mausoleum, in Riverside Cemetery, was also designed by architect Charles Brigham and patterned after the Temple of Minerva in Athens, Greece. Two urns flank the entranceway, and a Tiffany window casts a warm yellow and brown light on the interior.

2177 - The H. H. Rogers Mauseleum, Riverside Cemetery, Fairhaven, Mass.

Fort Phoenix

Fairhaven is situated on the east bank of the Acushnet River overlooking Buzzards Bay to the south. The Wampanoag people called the southernmost tip of the western shore Nolscot, meaning "place of the ledge." They came to Nolscot in the summer to hunt and fish. Later, American patriots constructed a fortress there to protect the town's harbor from British forces. Like its namesake, Fort Phoenix has lived through glory and decay and survived to rise again. Today, a national monument and state park, it is a symbol of the town's rich heritage and active present. Its grounds feature a public beach, picnic areas, hiking paths and striking vistas of Buzzards Bay and New Bedford Harbor. Not surprisingly, postcards have thoroughly documented the Fort's many faces over the last century.

Fort Phoenix, Water Front from the Pier, Fair Haven, Mass.

The old pavilion and environs, pictured here around 1900, hosted dances, clambakes, and entertainment. The fort's popularity grew fast. Summer clambakes and picnics were held in the Cedar Grove beginning in 1880. In 1886 the Union Street Railway Company put up the dance hall as a destination for would-be riders. Later, a concert hall was constructed just behind the 40-ft. beacon. As public bath houses were erected, restaurants and clam shacks opened, a raft was anchored offshore, and the area became a primary recreational resort.

In 1900, the Fairhaven Improvement Association erected 100 bath houses at the Fort Phoenix beach. The beach was leased by the streetcar company, which benefited greatly from the association's services. New bath houses, pavilions, and entertainment meant more people riding the trolley on warm summer days and nights. "Bathing parties were all the go," wrote the **Evening Standard** in July 1900, "and every class of resident was represented."

Fort Phoenix the Beach and Bath Houses, Fair Haven, Mass.

A ship entering New Bedford Harbor would have this view of the old fort circa 1900.

Beachgoers enjoy the raft moored just off the bath house pier, circa 1917. A big hit, the raft featured a horizontal chute at the bottom designed to temper the thrust of sliders as they hit the water. On opening day in 1916, the **Fairhaven Star** told the story of an unlucky lad who tried the chute standing up. When he reached the straightaway at the bottom, his feet slid from under him, he hit the back of his head on the chute, was knocked out, and sank when he struck the water. Saved by several of his fellow bathers, he was dragged onto the raft. The lifeguard launched his boat, retrieved the youngster, and revived him. Unable to walk for a while, the boy soon recovered enough to go home.

THE RAFT. FORT PHOENIX BATHING BEACH, FAIRHAVEN, MASS.

FORT PHOENIX BEACH, BATH HOUSE, FAIRHAVEN, MASS.

In 1916, the Union Street Railway erected new bath houses to encourage larger crowds. On opening day, July 8, 1916, the **Fairhaven Star** noted: "*The electric cars arrived in quartets, so crowded that women hung on the running boards, so anxious to get to the fort.... The beach was black with bathers.*" The newspaper called the structure, "*The Spanish castle.*" With its yellow-tinted concrete walls and red-tiled roof, it was "*as fine as any that can be found in the country.*"

The new pavilion at Fort Phoenix beach also opened in 1916. It too was constructed by the Union Street Railway and was located just west of the bath houses. Like earlier pavilions, it was multifunctional, with a large dance hall, concert area, dining hall, and adjacent open grounds for outings and clambakes.

THE PAVILION, FORT PHOENIX, FAIRHAVEN, MASS.

The new bath houses at Fort Phoenix could accommodate 1000 bathers. The colonnade and pier were topped with lights for evening dancing, and two large flood lamps were directed toward the water for evening swimming. The main building sparkled with a wax-coated maple floor that continued along the pier. Though designed for recreation, not for diving, the 160-foot pier invited dancers to take a plunge as part of their program. The bath houses, attached to the rear of the main building, were ideal—for 15 cents, the bather received a key and bath towel. Black bathing suits were also rented for 15 cents. There were 500 men's stalls, set up locker-room style, and 400 individual compartments for women.

On opening day, the **Fairhaven Star** noted one "daring fashion statement.... Her low cut suit...began just below the shoulders and its lower terminus was nowhere near on speaking terms with the young woman's knees."

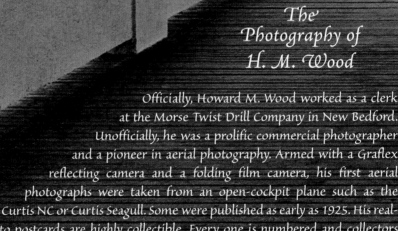

The Photography of H. M. Wood

Officially, Howard M. Wood worked as a clerk at the Morse Twist Drill Company in New Bedford. Unofficially, he was a prolific commercial photographer and a pioneer in aerial photography. Armed with a Graflex reflecting camera and a folding film camera, his first aerial photographs were taken from an open-cockpit plane such as the Curtis NC or Curtis Seagull. Some were published as early as 1925. His real-photo postcards are highly collectible. Every one is numbered and collectors have found cards numbering well into the 300s. Although Wood's postcards date from 1900 into the 1930s, most of his Fairhaven scenes are between 1905 and 1920. A deacon at the First Baptist Church and a member of the Providence Engineering Society Camera Club, he received many state and local photography awards.

New Bath House Pier , Fairhaven, Ma

H.M.Wood
148

Pavilion ~ Fort Phoenix.

Side view

The Fort Phoenix Pavilion was a summer gathering place for people from both sides of the Acushnet River. Between the 1880s and the 1920s, a 5-cent ride on the open-air trolley was the preferred mode of transportation for many city folks. Later, automobiles filled the parking areas as patrons poured in to enjoy clambakes, outings and entertainment.

Shown here circa 1916, the pavilion was severely damaged by hurricanes in 1938, 1944 and 1954, but continued to function as an entertainment facility until the early 1960s. In the mid-1960s, the rundown and boarded-up pavilion gave way to the beautification and expansion of the new Fort Phoenix State Park.

FORT PHOENIX PAVILION, FAIRHAVEN, MASS.   H.M.WOOD
171

VIEW AT FORT PHOENIX, FAIRHAVEN, MASS

WOOD 31

Ancient footpaths carve their way through the grounds of the old fort, circa 1910. The Fort Phoenix area had been used as a fortress long before the Revolutionary War. The site appears in a crude 1762 map of Old Dartmouth as "Fort Ruins" and was probably the remains of an Indian garrison.

Fairhaven rebels are credited with waging the first naval battle of the American Revolution, on May 14, 1775, just 27 days after the Battle of Concord and Lexington. A force of Fairhaven men aboard the sloop **Success**, led by Captain Nathaniel Pope, staged a surprise attack in Vineyard Sound against the British sloop-of-war **Falcon**. After a brief fight, they took a number of prisoners, including 11 officers, but were back at anchor in home port "before meeting time." In 1777, local patriots built a fortification here and referred to it as the fort at Nolscot. It was armed with 11 cannons captured by junior naval officer John Paul Jones.

Fort Phoenix - Fairhaven, Mass.

MAJOR FEARING MEMORIAL, FAIRHAVEN, MASS.

WOOD 32

In September 1778, after burning Bedford Village and torching homes from Acushnet to Sconticut Neck, the British captured the fort after the local militia, abandoned by their commander, cut and ran. Two days later, the British returned to Fairhaven Village and marched south, pillaging and burning homes along the way. A young officer from Wareham, Major Israel Fearing, took charge of the demoralized men, inviting those willing to fight to post themselves just outside the fort. Fearing recharged his trembling troops by threatening to shoot any deserters. The troops responded and met the advancing enemy with a ferocious volley of musket fire. The British fled and the next morning sailed to Martha's Vineyard to further pillage and terrorize.

The Fairhaven Improvement Association cleaned the grounds around the fort and restored and mounted the abandoned Civil War cannons in 1886. They set the Fearing Boulder in place in 1904.

A 21845   Interior of Fort Phoenix Fairhaven, Mass.

Fort Phenix Fairhaven Mass.

Two views of the fort, circa 1910, show the ammunition magazine (topped with a grassy knoll), stone walls, and expanded ramparts that shored up the garrison during the Civil War. Fort Phoenix, which had been rebuilt in 1781, was put in order in 1861, and three companies were stationed there for home defense. It was feared that rebel cruisers might visit New Bedford Harbor as the British had done during both the Revolutionary War and the War of 1812. Six 24-pound cannons were mounted on the parapet and new barracks were built. After the war, a noncommissioned officer was stationed at the fort as custodian. He and his wife moved into the vacated tenant house, stored hay in the barracks, and kept livestock. In 1876, the government determined that the fort had outlived its usefulness, and deactivated it.

A 21844 Old Fort Phoenix, Fairhaven, Mass.

Fort Phoenix, near New Bedford, Mass.

Left to the elements between 1876 and 1885, the abandoned fort grew desolate and decrepit. Several of the old cannons were given away, property vandalized or stolen, and the bunkers nearly destroyed. Sometime around 1880, a couple named Dean built a one-room house (shown in these two postcards, circa 1910) just east of the present Fearing Boulder. Old photographs show that the ruins provided ample feeding grounds for the couple's chicken roost. In 1885, the Fairhaven Improvement Association mounted the cannons in suitable carriages to improve the appearance of fort. Though still in the possession of the government, the fort was maintained by the Town of Fairhaven—even as the Deans tended their poultry. By 1900, the Deans had moved on. They were succeeded by a number of people who also used the fort as a residence.

Fort Phenix Fairhaven Mass.

New Bedford Harbor from Port Phoenix.

A view from the ramparts shows the Nantucket Steamship Company ferry **Gay Head** crossing the harbor at Palmer's Island. The **Gay Head** was the last of the wooden steamers of the Island steamship line.

When World War I erupted, the fort played no official part except as a place for drilling State Guard Companies. On the day of the signing of the Armistice in 1918, a group that had gathered at the fort to celebrate set fire to the grounds, leaving no building standing. In 1925 the federal government placed Fort Phoenix on the surplus list and put it up for sale at $5,000. Neither the county nor the state wanted it, and the town couldn't afford it. In 1926, just as the property was in danger of being transferred to developers, Lady Fairhaven came to its rescue. Lady Fairhaven was Mrs. Cara Leland Broughton, daughter of H. H. Rogers. Citing her father's love of the fort, she bought the 2.5-acre historic site and presented it to the town for use as a park.

Fort Phoenix Looking South from Inside Fairhaven, Mass. 214659

ROAD TO FT. PHOENIX, FAIRHAVEN, M

In this postcard, circa 1910, the end of Fort Street leading to Fort Phoenix is little more than a dirt path. The sign for Grimshaw's Famous Clambakes can be seen between the trees in the cedar grove on the left. Mr. and Mrs. William C. Grimshaw began serving clambakes at Fort Phoenix in 1884 and continued until they sold out in 1944. The business operated until the late 1960s.

The ferry **Fairhaven** steams toward New Bedford, circa 1914. From 1833 to 1929, ferries transported about eight million passengers between Fairhaven and New Bedford. On the day this vessel began its run in 1896, 3000 tickets were sold. The **Fairhaven** made 19 round trips a day in its heyday and was replaced in 1916. The ferry service was always popular with passengers, even until its final days in 1929. When the ferry's owner, the Fairhaven Branch Railroad, tried to stop the service and discourage passenger usage with awkward schedules, people protested. However, when freight service along the Old Colony Line to the Cape was discontinued, passenger service alone could not keep the ferry solvent.

FERRYBOAT "FAIRHAVEN"

On the Waterfront

At the mouth of the Acushnet River, Fairhaven and New Bedford share one of New England's oldest and most illustrious deep-water ports. For three centuries the port has launched whaling, fishing and merchant fleets that have, at various intervals, reigned supreme in the annals of American maritime history. Fairhaven is noted for her many shipyards which thrive today in the service and repair of all types of vessels. The views featured here include landmarks such as lighthouses and bridges, rustic waterfront views, ferries, hurricane scenes and more.

H.M.Wood
113

FAIRHAVEN WATERFONT

McGee's
PHOTO SUPPLY

Wharves & Shipyards

This photo postcard shows the Fairhaven waterfront around 1951. The three main wharves are, from left to right, Kelley's (formerly Old South Wharf), Union, and Hathaway Braley (formerly Railroad Wharf). The small wharf at far left is Mullen's Wharf (formerly Delano's or Old North Wharf).

Old South Wharf dates to before the Revolution and is one of the oldest existing wharves in the country. From here, whalers and merchant ships sailed the globe. In its history, the wharf was home to coopers, blacksmiths, tinsmiths, cabinet makers, shipwrights, taverns and bakeries. It was also home to Fairhaven's first newspaper, the **Bristol Gazette**, and to Courtland Fairchild's hen house.

1172 Yachts Fitting out Fairhaven Mass

Kelley's Wharf (far left) and Shipyard seen from the air around 1960. Union Wharf is just right of center.

Union Wharf, built in 1804, was the primary dock for Fairhaven's whaling fleet. The **Fairhaven Star** wrote, "Bustling clerks, bestocked and bewhiskered whaling princes, fine ladies in balloon skirts, ladies not so fine, swearing and sweating stevedores and noisy youngsters flocked there to transact business. The smells, the noises and usual scenes created a delightful atmosphere that will never exist again." In 1887, Henry H. Rogers came into possession of the wharf and ran pipes through it to outflow the town's new sewer system. Rogers' family sold it to the Iron Foundry in 1917, which sold it to Morse Twist Drill, for use as fuel storage. In 1926, the town reclaimed the wharf by eminent domain. Soon it became home to various fishing sheds, private businesses, Casey's Boat Building Company, Babbitt Brothers, and Keith Ice Cream Company.

UNION WHARF, FAIRHAVEN, MASS.   H.M.WOOD
                                                    49

In 1926, Peirce and Kilburn Shipyard moved from New Bedford to property on Fort Street that once housed a candle works, a sperm oil refinery, and the Atlas Tack Company. The new yard installed a marine railway system capable of hauling out large steamships. By 1942, Peirce and Kilburn launched the 98-foot **Potomska**, which they claimed was the nation's biggest fishing dragger. In the 1950s, Peirce and Kilburn began manufacturing new, "unsinkable" fiberglass boats and was among the first to use the locomotive roundhouse for yacht storage. With steam-heated storage sheds and multiple tracks, the round house was the largest facility of its kind between Bristol, Connecticut and Boston. Today, the yard is known as Fairhaven Shipyard.

This postcard shows sailing vessels wrapped for winter storage at Peirce and Kilburn, circa 1940s.

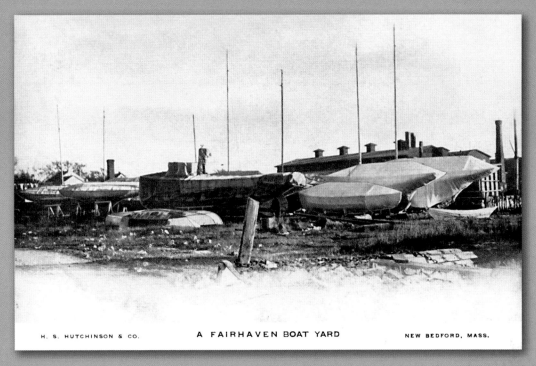

H. S. HUTCHINSON & CO.   A FAIRHAVEN BOAT YARD   NEW BEDFORD, MASS.

Major Casey's boatyard was moved to the basin between the Union and Hathaway Braley wharves in 1927. Casey designed many boats, including lifeboats for Admiral Perry's ship **Roosevelt**, which made the North Pole expedition in 1908. He later designed and built speedboats for the government in World War I. During Prohibition, rumrunners used Casey's boats because they were among the few that could outrun the feds. From 1926 to 1934, the Casey yard turned out 121 boats ranging from 22 to 65 feet. In World War II, it produced nineteen 105-foot rescue boats for the U.S. Army and several draggers for the fishing fleet.

A fishing schooner on the "ways" at Fairhaven Marine Railway, around 1910. Located between Union Wharf and Railroad Wharf, this yard would later become Casey's Boat Yard.

H. S. HUTCHINSON & CO   MARINE RAILWAY, FAIRHAVEN   NEW BEDFORD, MASS.

NEW BEDFORD FROM THE AIR, NEW BEDFORD, MASS.

View of New Bedford Harbor from Fairhaven, circa 1938, showing the wharf at Peirce and Kilburn at lower left. Because of the its proximity to the fertile fishing grounds on Georges Banks, the port of New Bedford (including Fairhaven) began to prosper. By 1945, its fishing industry was worth $10 million. As the port expanded, facilities improved. By 1948, 1400 fishermen worked 265 vessels, and 27 fillet houses employed 550 people.

A growing fleet of draggers lay over at Hathaway Braley Wharf, in the 1950s. At this time, Hathaway Braley Machine Company, one of the best-equipped marine and engineering facilities in the country, designed and repaired much of the heavy hoisting machinery used by the fleet. Their success began in 1919 when Eli Hathaway developed the first two-headed winch. His winches used steel drums and cables, allowing the use of stronger and heavier fishing gear, which gave birth to the modern dragger.

Fishing Boats, Fairhaven Harbor, Mass.

The dragger **The Friars** was ravaged by Hurricane Carol in 1954 and left to rot along Union Wharf for at least six years. The 84-foot eastern-rigged vessel, built in Friendship, Maine, in 1928, was rescued by William Q. MacLean, who spent $40,000 to repair and refit her for lobstering and quahogging. The back of the postcard reads: "Survivor of an attack by German Submarine in World War II."

The seaplane tied up along the marina near the Coast Guard Auxiliary Wharf belongs to Norman Gingrass, a Mattapoisett native who operated a daily passenger service to Cuttyhunk for over 30 years. Gingrass' service was a lifeline to the small, rustic island. In addition to ferrying schoolchildren, honeymooners and tourists, he transported cargo, delivered mail and assisted rescue operations.

Marina Scene, Fairhaven, Mass.

View from Kelley's Wharf looking east toward the town, circa 1910. Ahira Kelley, a fishing schooner captain, purchased the Old South Wharf in 1864, renaming it after himself. In the foreground are codfish drying racks called fish flakes. Kelley's fish processing enterprise was so profitable that he began importing codfish from Nova Scotia. He sold under the name "Fine As Can Be."

KELLEY'S WHARF, FAIRHAVE

In the early 1900s, Kelley's went into the ship repair business but continued fishing, particularly for cod. In the 1920s, they started building hydroplanes (racing boats), which were later sold around the world as "Baby Whales." Around 1935, Kelley's quit both the racing boat and the fishing business to concentrate on ship repair, becoming one of the busiest yards on the East Coast during World War II. At that time it employed about 150 men, who worked on everything from fishing boats and pleasure craft to mine sweepers. After the war, Kelley's began building 40-foot boats called mackerel seiners. Today, the yard still services and repairs fishing boats and other ships.

MASS.

H.M.WOOD
48

ACROSS THE HARBOR, FAIRHAVEN, MASS.   WOOD 35

Harbor Views

View of New Bedford Harbor from the vicinity of Fort Phoenix, circa 1910.

The hurricane barrier around New Bedford Harbor, built between 1962 and 1965 at a cost of $18.5 million, stretches more than 3.5 miles—4500 feet across the entrance to the harbor, 9800 feet along the southeast shore of New Bedford, and 2100 feet along the Fort Phoenix shore. It was the first hurricane-protection structure in the Western Hemisphere built to close off an entire harbor. In 1965, it was nominated by the American Society of Civil Engineers as one of the outstanding feats of civil engineering.

Built in 1902, the **Uncatena** was the first steel-hulled ferry used by the New Bedford, Martha's Vineyard and Nantucket Steamboat Company. The ship could carry six cars and was the first steamship of the line to be equipped with an electric searchlight. Ferry boats from New Bedford Harbor served the islands continuously from the 1830s until 1960, after which the Nantucket Steamship Authority moved to Woods Hole. Today, the Fairhaven shipyards continue to serve as repair facilities for the ferries.

In this 1950s view from Poverty Point (Oxford Village) looking south, a sailor paddles his dinghy toward the mother ship—a pleasure boat moored north of the New Bedford-Fairhaven Bridge.

Cogshall St. Bridge, Bristol & Grinell Mills, New Bedford, Mass.

Bridges & Lighthouses

The Coggeshall Street Bridge connects the northern sections of New Bedford and Fairhaven. In the background are the Columbia, Bennett and Soule textile mills—three of more than 50 textile operations that sprawled throughout the city. With the construction of this bridge in 1892, North Fairhaven was now within walking distance of New Bedford's fast-growing industrial workplace. As a result, a more densely-populated neighborhood of multi-family dwellings arose in the northern sector to house the new working class.

This 1950s photo card shows the entire length of the New Bedford-Fairhaven Bridge, touching Fish Island and Pope's Island along the way. It was taken from the roof of the New Bedford Hotel on Pleasant Street.

NEW BEDFORD - FAIRHAVEN, BRIDGE

McGee's
PHOTO SUPPLY

Old New Bedford and Fairhaven Bridge. Had over 100 years service.

The first roadway bridge connecting New Bedford and Fairhaven, via Fish Island, was built around 1800. It lasted 100 years, though the wooden draw was rebuilt several times. This draw was built in 1870, replacing one destroyed by the Gale of 1869. Like earlier bridges, it required a toll to cross. Because of the toll, the delays, and the crudeness of early modes of transportation, residents often preferred to cross the river by ferry. "The bridge is still thought by many to be a great public damage," wrote historian Daniel Ricketson in 1858. "It…is questionable whether it accommodates the public better than might be done by the ferry boats; and, the value of our harbor, as well as the beauty of the river, is much impaired by it."

The "new" New Bedford-Fairhaven Bridge was completed in 1902. The open-air trolley crossing the swing-span bridge was used specifically on the Fort Phoenix line during the summer.

NEW BEDFORD AND FAIRHAVEN BRIDGE, NEW BEDFORD, MASS.

2134 Popes Island and Fairhaven Bridge, New Bedford, Mass

These two views of the New Bedford-Fairhaven Bridge were taken from the New Bedford Yacht Club located on Pope's Island, circa 1906. The top view looks east toward Fairhaven; the bottom view looks west toward Fish Island. The area of blue water in the foreground of both views (as well as the yacht club itself) would later be filled to create a city park, greatly enlarging Pope's Island. Although the old bridge roadway zig-zagged its way to a small peninsula on the Fairhaven shoreline at Bridge Street, Henry H. Rogers, appearing at City Council meetings in New Bedford, fought Mayor Charles S. Ashley and the city council to have the new roadway built in a straight line from Pope's Island. It's likely that he had already picked out a spot for his envisioned high school (built in 1906) and planned to showcase it to travelers entering the town via the bridge. Rogers later acquired the land north and south of the road leading off the bridge and gave it to the town.

2003 - New Bedford and Fairhaven Bridge

Palmer Island Light House, New Bedford, Mass.

61855

Palmer's Island is a 46,000 square-foot spit of land at the edge of the inner harbor. Its historic lighthouse is a 24-foot, rubblestone tower built in 1849. An 1850 inspection noted, "The dome of the lantern…was just as black as could be—caused by burning Mr. Rodman's lamp with whale oil." In the 1860s, a hotel and dance hall were built on the island. The hotel was a favorite stop for whalers, and illegal activity prompted its closing about 1890. The lighthouse was restored in 1999 and still shines today.

Butler Flats lighthouse, at the entrance to the outer harbor, was built in 1898 by F. Hopkinson Smith, builder of the Statue of Liberty's foundation. Set in shallow water with a mud floor, it was a construction challenge. In April 1898, keeper Amos Baker, Jr. wrote, "At 7AM took charge of Butler Flats Lighthouse. . . . The lighthouse is new but found it very wet and leaky and very dirty and everything topsy turvy."

Butler Flats Light, New Bedford, Mass.

Around the Town

This chapter features random sights around town. There are landmarks, businesses, industries, streets, houses, schools, churches, trains, trolleys and hurricanes. Often, postcards are serious works of art that represent important places or beautiful landscapes. Sometimes, however, they simply represent an individual's desire to show off a new business or home or photographic prowess. In this section, then, as well as throughout the book, we find artful landscapes and street scenes by H. M. Wood, fanciful, neo-modern interiors intended to promote a business, and somewhat crude darkroom innovations printed on photographic paper created purely for personal pleasure. While they don't represent a total picture of the town, they give us a graphic microcosm, sure to bring a smile.

BRIDGE DINER

"AT YOUR SERVICE"

BRIDGE SEA GRILL

BRIDGE DINER

NEW BEDFORD & FAIRHAVEN BRIDGE, NEW BEDFORD, MASS.

The landmark Bridge Diner, located on Pope's Island near the town line, opened in 1940. Typical of American roadside diners, it was designed in the classic Art Deco style and served the fast food of the day.

Macomber's Variety Store, a fixture on Sconticut Neck Road since 1926, could meet all grocery needs—deli meats, canned goods, milk and candy. It was also one of the first gas stations in Fairhaven. The old-time gravity pump (which functioned by pumping gasoline into a glass globe atop the pump then relying on gravity to push it through the hose) is not visible in the photo but you can see the kerosene pump on the porch. Mr. and Mrs. Macomber lived above the store. Their rumble-seat Chevy in the foreground is still in service. The Macombers sold the store in the 1950s to the Simmons family. Tony Simmons sold the business in 1967 to the Jacksons. Today, you can still get milk and candy at Jackson's Variety.

Macomber's Variety Store and Post Office, East Fairhaven, Mass.

MACOMBER'S VARIETY STORE

Dance Pavilion, Pope Beach, East Fairhaven, Mass.

The Dance Pavilion at Pope Beach was originally built in the 1870s as a retreat dormitory for Jesuit priests and seminary students from Boston College. According to historian Mabel Porter, who could not authenticate the story, "One Mrs. Baker, a New Bedford widow, fell in love with a priest, one of the officials of the College, and as some satisfaction to her soul proposed to buy the West farm for the College. This the priest accepted, and for many years, this tract was known as the Catholic Place. [The pavilion] was occupied every summer by groups of student priests. I well remember them tramping the roads and playing ball, never [bothering] anyone." In 1901, the dormitory was sold and converted to a dance hall, that was said to have "the finest dance floor in the area."

Cottages at Pope Beach look out on Priests' Cove, Sconticut Neck. The area around the pavilion soon gave way to summer cottages and year-round homes. Most of them were destroyed in the Hurricane of 1938.

Pope Beach, East Fairhaven, Mass.

WORKS OF THE ATLAS TACK COMPANY, FAIRHAVEN, MASS., U. S. A.

In 1903, historian James Gillingham called Atlas Tack Company "the largest and best-equipped tack mill in the world," employing 450 people and exporting worldwide. In 1936, the company was bought by a syndicate of outside interests that diversified production. With new product the company showed periods of growth, but it was also plagued by labor strife, lawsuits, mismanagement and environmental catastrophe. A fire in 1979 and dwindling productivity brought an end to the world's oldest tack maker in June 1985.

Designed by Charles Brigham and completed in 1893, the Millicent Library is in the early Italian Renaissance style, with a terra-cotta-trimmed granite exterior and a red slate roof. In 1968, the town financed an addition with federal grants and contributions from several Rogers descendants.

2040 Millicent Library, Fairhaven, Mass.

Peter Murray was a 23-old Scottish immigrant in the employ of Walter Windsor when he developed the Windsor Pink carnation in 1904. The flower was a great success, enabling Murray to open this store at 164 Washington Street. In 1906, a New York company paid Murray $16,000 for a single flower. In 1911, the Windsor Pink was chosen as the coronation flower for England's Queen Mary and soon became the rage of Britain.

Riverside Cemetery was established on 44 acres of farmland by Warren Delano II, grandfather of President Franklin Delano Roosevelt. Developed by Delano's personal groundskeepers and featuring mausoleums by architects Richard Morris Hunt and Charles Brigham, Riverside was said to be one of the most beautiful garden cemeteries in the country at the time.

2215 - The Van Nostrand Residence,
Fairhaven, Mass.

The Alonzo G. Van Nostrand House at one Main Street was built in 1912. Van Nostrand was a Boston native whose family's fortune came from the Bunker Hill Brewery in Charlestown, makers of P & B Ale. Unfortunately, the business took a fatal hit from the Prohibition Act of 1920. Van Nostrand used his free time to develop gardens around his house. He bought several adjacent properties and expanded his gardens, which became town attractions in early summer. When Van Nostrand died in 1923, his son, William, took over the 16-room house and gardens and lived there with his wife Elizabeth until 1958. Today, the home is a bed & breakfast inn.

The Levasseur house was designed by New Bedford architect Louis E. Destremps at a cost of $60,000 in 1910. In 1933, the house was moved 120 feet because it stood in the direct path of the new federal highway (Route 6). A fire of suspicious origin destroyed the building in the 1970s.

2221 - The Levasseur House, Fairhaven, Mass.

Some of the town's grandest houses are on the east bank of the outer harbor. Rogers' mansion is at center.

These houses on Huttleston Avenue (near Adams Street) were built by Henry H. Rogers in 1908 during his tenure as Superintendent of Streets. The town created that office in 1890, and six years later Rogers was appointed to the post at an annual salary of $1. As street czar, he laid out new streets, paved sidewalks, installed curbs, extended and improved older streets, built Cushman Park and the Water Works, and opened up new areas for development. Since the town's annual budget for street work was just $3,000, Rogers financed all surplus expenses.

Churches & Schools

Built in 1841 as the Centre Congregational Church, the Greek Revival building was sold in 1846 to the Centre Methodist Episcopal Church. The clock tower was the official timekeeper for residents for over 50 years.

Robert Bruce's 30-foot-tall "Good Shepherd" ambles across the rear wall of the Church of the Good Shepherd Episcopal Church in North Fairhaven. Completed in 1972, the fresco was created with egg tempera and charcoal over a meticulously prepared bath of slaked lime, sand and various pigments. Bruce's vision of the shepherd, shaped from boyhood experiences caring for sheep on his father's Topeka, Kansas farm, is one of a strong, compassionate peasant living under the stars rather than the aged shepherd shown in most renderings.

The Trinity Lutheran Church was organized by the town's Norwegian community, who first arrived in the area in the 1920s to take part in the fishing industry. This building was dedicated in 1979.

Congregational Church, Fairhaven, Mass.

The Congregational Church was built in 1844 with a 100-foot wooden spire that was used as a navigational aid by whalers sailing into the harbor. The spire was destroyed in the Gale of 1869.

Established in 1852, the Old High School focused on college preparation. In its first year, there were 95 applicants, of which 70 were admitted, including Henry H. Rogers. At a class reunion in 1892, Rogers recalled, "I was the first to be flogged in the school, and aside from the disgrace, I had to furnish the rod." Rogers had been sent out by the Master to find a rod to punish a girl with. He returned with a small stick. The Master laughed but sent him out again. This time, he returned with a twig. No longer laughing, the Master kept him after school, whereupon he was sent out to find a rod to whip a boy with. "I found the rod, and true to the laws of compensation, the rod found me." Originally built as a chapel by the Methodist Episcopal Church in 1830, the building was razed in 1920.

2002 The Old High School, Fairhaven, Mass.

Fairhaven High School, Fairhaven, Mass.

According to an article in **New England Magazine** in 1907, "At first view one is impelled to wonder if enough pupils to fill it can be found in all Fairhaven....The exterior is imposing from its size and disposition of parts, and inspection of the interior quickly reveals how far Americans have travelled from the educational ideal, once embodied in 'the little red schoolhouse.'" The high school was designed by architect Charles Brigham, born in Watertown in 1841. With John Sturgis of Boston, Brigham designed many homes in Boston's Back Bay and in Newport, Rhode Island. Outside Fairhaven, his most prominent structures include the Church of the Advent on Brimmer Street in Boston, wings on the State House, the imposing Christian Science Temple on Massachusetts Avenue, and the New Bedford Institution for Savings.

Students take a break at the high school cafeteria, circa 1907.

Parish House, Roger's Memorial Church.   Fairhaven, Mass.

This Elizabethan Tudor-style cottage is not the Unitarian Church Parish House but the Parsonage, or Manse. The two buildings, designed by Charles Brigham, are often confused.

The Parish House dining hall features three sets of eight-foot folding entrance doors leading into the entertainment room. Its ceiling is trussed with great oak beams decorated in Gothic tracery. At its dedication in 1903, a reporter wrote, "Those who were fortunate enough to be present on this occasion were lost in the wonder of the work of the skilled artist and artisan….The equal of the beautiful carving in oak around doors and mantel and windows and wall is seldom seen by the average mortal. The white hunter limestone beautifully contrasted with the darker finish of the interior, and the sun's rays, as they shone through the many colors of glass and tracery windows, gave additional beauty to it." Today, the Parish House is used as a school, library and office.

9107 Dining-Room, Parish House, Unitarian Memorial Church, Fairhaven, Mass.

Less than five years after the Rogers School was built, Henry H. Rogers became unhappy with the discoloration and white streaks on the outer brick walls and ordered the brick replaced. Fifty thousand fine-pressed, superior-quality bricks, all even in size and a rich dark red, were shipped in at a cost of $50 per thousand. Work began in May 1890, as skilled masons gradually removed and inserted new brick. Great pains were taken to ensure a perfect finish. To protect the new brick, straw was placed between every course in the pile. The job was expected to take five months but lasted nearly eight. Delays were caused by problems such as the need to make new plans for window trimmings and arches, the selectmen's decision to place a terra-cotta tablet with the school's name below the clock face, and the defection of six masons because of trouble with the boss.

Postcard

Roger's School.   Fairhaven Mass.

Architect Charles Brigham's "crowning achievement, not only at Fairhaven but in his professional career, yet remains to be noticed—the Unitarian Church, with its immediate adjuncts. Beautiful beyond anything yet attempted in New England church architecture, it stands in all its fair proportions a lasting testimonial to the abiding love and reverence of a son for his mother, and of the genius of the architects who translated that love into soaring tower and richly sculptured line, so wisely and so well." (**New England Magazine**, 1907)

2034 Unitarian Memorial Church, Fairhaven, Mass.

This is a rare view of the interior of the first St. Joseph's Church, built in 1905. For 20 years the building also housed the St. Joseph's parochial school. In 1925, a new church (right) was built and the old church was used exclusively as the school. It was torn down in 1965 when a new school was built.

St. Joseph Church in Fairhaven,

After the Centre Methodist Episcopal Church (page 68) was destroyed by fire in January 1946, this new church was constructed on the same property, with a similar design but without a steeple, in 1947.

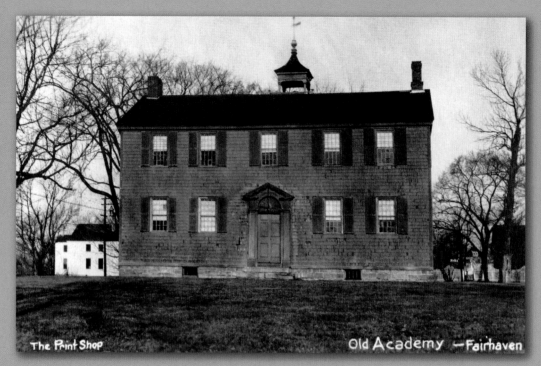

Built circa 1798, the New Bedford Academy (Fairhaven was at the time part of New Bedford), was a private school for advanced pupils until 1852, when Fairhaven's first high school was built. In 1906, Rogers bought the school and moved it from its location diagonally across the avenue from the current high school to the high school's north lawn, where it remains in the care of the Fairhaven Historical Commission.

Sacred Hearts Academy, an all-girls school, was established in 1911 by 50 French-Canadian families who had met in 1907 at the Howland House, next door, to establish the Sacred Hearts Parish.

OXFORD SCHOOL, Fairhaven, Mass.

The Oxford Elementary School was constructed in 1896 in North Fairhaven. With only four rooms, it was quickly outgrown by its neighborhood, which was rapidly expanding because of the development of the textile mills in New Bedford, and four more rooms had to be built in 1914. Housed in the cupola atop the school is Revere bell number 10, forged in 1790 by the Boston silversmith, Paul Revere.

The Job C. Tripp Elementary School on Green Street was built in 1918 and named for one of the town's most dedicated public servants. Job Tripp served Fairhaven in many capacities, including 50 years on the School Committee, president of the Improvement Association, postmaster, library trustee and Sunday school superintendent. A former clerk for Charles W. Morgan, he later opened his own whaling firm in town.

A 21849 Fort Street, Fairhaven, Mass.

Streets & Houses

Many of today's streets are yesterday's pathways, blazed by foot and horsecart, now covered by asphalt. Here, the horse and wagon heading south on Fort Street toward Fort Phoenix, leave room for a trolley that may be right on its heels—filled with people seeking sunshine at the seashore.

Once-narrow, elm-shaded Centre Street is captured in this photo postcard. A sliver of the Centre Methodist Church can be seen at left, and the Millicent Library is at right.

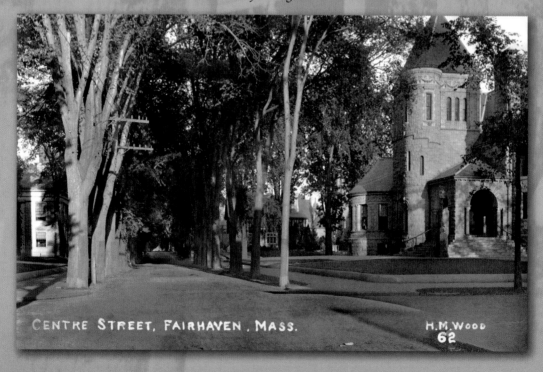

CENTRE STREET, FAIRHAVEN, MASS.   H.M.WOOD 62

UNION STREET, FAIRHAVEN, MASS.

H.M.WOOD 46

Union Street, circa 1905, looking west from Chestnut Street. Much of Fairhaven town center, except for the waterfront area, was purchased by the Rotch Family in 1765 and held by them for 67 years without development. It is believed that the property (86.5 acres) was held for investment purposes—perhaps to develop products (either manufactured or farmed) for export to his native Nantucket. For this reason, most houses and streets in Fairhaven date between 1830 and 1890, while closer to the waterfront they date from 1770 to 1830. Also, because the town was over-ripe for growth at the time, the townspeople were able to quickly lay out beautifully designed streets with many large houses on relatively small lots. Fairhaven retains this character today.

Green Street looking north from South Street, circa 1910. Green Street was accepted as a throughway in 1832, running from Abner Vincent's store (Spring Street) to Rotch's land (South Street).

1118 H. S. HUTCHINSON & CO.   GREEN STREET, FAIRHAVEN   NEW BEDFORD, MASS.

WALNUT ST.
FAIRHAVEN, MASS.

Fairhaven has had a long romance with trees—generously gracing its center with virulent New England hardwood. The Fairhaven Improvement Association and the Superintendent of Streets (Rogers and his successor John I. Bryant) spent considerable resources planning, developing and maintaining the town's byways. According to town historian Mabel Knipe, "When Mr. Rogers sent thousands of trees to line the new streets—John I. Bryant became their guardian and protector. Woe be to the horses who tore the leaves off Rogers' trees—or the errant citizen who tied his horse to a trunk and mutilated the bark!" Bryant annually berated owners of horses that ate the leaves off the trees, and cried aloud at the Association meetings begging parents to keep their offspring from digging their heels into the newly laid street macadam.

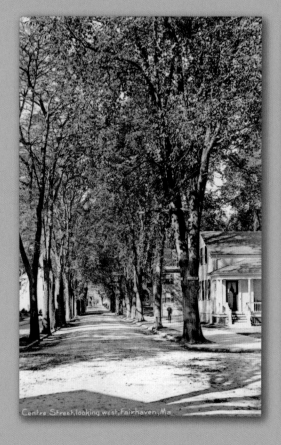

Centre Street, looking west, Fairhaven, Ma

A 21858 Centre Street, looking East, Fairhaven, Mass.

On September 14, 1944, hurricane winds exceeding 100-mph whipped through the region. Many of the old elm trees lining the center streets were uprooted during the storm, causing severe damage to property and utilities. In New Bedford and Fairhaven, it was estimated that more than 3000 mature trees were destroyed.

GREEN ST., FAIRHAVEN, MASS.

WOOD 11

HUTTLESTON AVE., FAIRHAVE

Huttleston Avenue was part of Rogers' plan for a grand entrance into Fairhaven. Coming off the bridge from New Bedford, the traveler passed the magnificent high school and proceeded along the beautifully manicured boulevard. At the time of this photograph, circa 1910, Huttleston Avenue was only three blocks long, terminating at Adams Street, where the Levasseur House can be seen in the distance. When this picture was taken, circa 1912, there weren't enough cars on the road to disturb anyone on horseback out for a mid-day ride. Though Rogers didn't live to see it, he would have undoubtedly been pleased with the Huttleston Avenue's extension and merger into Washington Street and its incorporation into U.S. Route 6 in 1933.

MASS.

H.M. WOOD
44

A Typical New England Doorway.

Published by J. G. Tirrell, New Bedford, Mass.

The old Jenney house, built in 1764, was the last remaining gambrel in Fairhaven Village. Located on the present site of the George H. Taber Lodge, it was occupied by John Taber, an ironsmith, and survived the British invasion in 1778. Horatio Jenney sold it to Henry H. Rogers, who demolished it in 1900 to make way for the Masonic Block.

The Proctor House was the first house built on the 20-Acre Purchase, the nucleus of Fairhaven Village. Built in 1760 at the foot of Washington Street, it was sold to Samuel Proctor in 1774 and served as a residence and a cooper shop. In 1904, Henry B. Worth called it one of the six finest houses in Old Dartmouth from that early period. The house was razed in 1932.

PROCTOR HOUSE.
BUILT ABOUT 1760.   FAIRHAVEN.   MASS.

MONASTERY OF THE SACRED HEARTS, FAIRHAVEN
Formerly Residence of Theodore Thomas
H. S. HUTCHINSON & CO.   NEW BEDFORD, MASS.

In 1905, the Fathers of the Sacred Hearts purchased this house for use as a monastery. Located at Spring and Adams Street, it was formerly the summer residence of celebrated musician Theodore Thomas, the "father of the American Symphony Orchestra." It later became the rectory of St. Joseph's Parish.

Ezekiel Sawin, first president of the National Bank of Fairhaven, erected this Greek Revival Mansion in 1840. In 1867, the house was purchased by Weston Howland, the man who distilled kerosene from coal in 1858, one year before the discovery of petroleum in Pennsylvania. In 1860, Howland discovered the secret of refining petroleum to a degree suitable for burning in lamps. Soon, Howland's method became known, leading the Standard Oil Company, with Rogers in the front office, to put him and other small companies out of business in 1877.

1208   Weston Howland House   Fairhaven, Mass.

No 7 Oxford St. Dec 27- 1906

This cottage is one of the more nondescript dwellings in Oxford Village, the town's oldest neighborhood. Lined with 18th-century homes nestled along ancient streets, Oxford was developed on a tiny peninsula jutting into the Acushnet River. The original 6-acre parcel of land was sold to Elnathan Eldredge in 1760. Eldredge divided the land into 30 house lots, which he sold mostly to mariners. At the foot of Oxford Street, Eldredge built a wharf and a store, and began dealing in West India goods, groceries and household items. The name "Oxford" was used for the first time in a 1773 deed. Before that, the village was referred to as "Ye Little Town at Ye Foot of William Woods's Homestead" and later as "Uppertown."

The Joseph S. Borden House, at Main and Coggeshall streets, is situated just north of Oxford Village.

54273 The Homestead, Fairhaven, Mass.

The "Homestead," built circa 1812 and located on north Main Street, was opened to summer boarders by its owner, E. H. Hatch. This photograph was taken around 1890. North Fairhaven, called Oxford, was primarily farmland at this time, but things began to change in the mid-1890s. After the Coggeshall Street Bridge was completed in 1892, North Fairhaven's landscape was carved up by the town and by developers who would build homes for families working in the nearby New Bedford mills.

The Kopper Kettle Guest House, located directly across from Fairhaven High School on Huttleston Avenue, provided a home-like atmosphere for travelers in the 1940s. Olive LaRiviera was the proprietor.

THE KOPPER KETTLE GUEST HOUSE, 41 Huttleston Ave., U. S. Route 6, Fairhaven, Mass

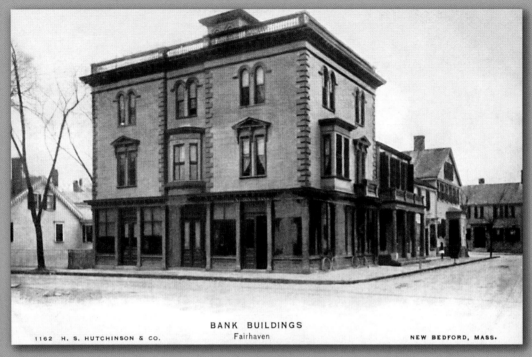

BANK BUILDINGS
Fairhaven

1162 H. S. HUTCHINSON & CO.   NEW BEDFORD, MASS.

Business & Industry

For 45 years, the National Bank of Fairhaven and the Fairhaven Institution for Savings shared the small brick building directly behind this large three-story building, which was built in 1860 by Noah Stoddard. The National Bank bought and moved into this building in 1877 and sold the smaller one to its former tenant, the Institution for Savings. The two banks once had a close relationship—they were incorporated in 1831–1832, and Ezekiel Sawin was elected president of both.

The Bridge Diner was located on Pope's Island, midway between New Bedford and Fairhaven, on U.S. Route 6. Yesterday's fast-food restaurants and diners served light snacks and full-course dinners.

NEW BRIDGE DINER ON THE NEW BEDFORD-FAIRHAVEN BRIDGE

THE CHICKEN HOUSE - FAIRHAVEN, MASS.

In the 1930s, Bert Owen operated a small tea room next to his chicken farm on Route 6 in East Fairhaven. The idea to serve fresh-raised chicken in his tea room gave birth to the Chicken House Restaurant. One of the Owens' more famous patrons was film and radio star Rudy Vallee, who loved their chicken pie.

Fairhaven was home to several clambake connoisseurs—Grimshaw, Whitfield, and Brown were perhaps the best known. Clambakes at Brown's Pavilion were usually family affairs. The spacious grounds and waterfront location on Sconticut Neck were ideal. While parents talked and ate at picnic tables sprawled across the front lawn, kids played ball, went swimming, or just ran wild. Serving clams from Maine, quahogs from Sconticut Neck, and sweet corn from local farms, the Brown family rarely advertised—guests returned by reservation.

JO-BROWN'S CLAMBAKE PAVILION
SCONTICUT NK.

The Fairhaven Ice Company was established in 1842 by William Eldridge and George Stevens. It was bought by L. S. Clark in 1909. Around the time of this photograph, in 1912, the **Fairhaven Star** reported that Clark's houses "are filled with 4500 tons of clean ice and he expects to be able to serve the Fairhaven people promptly this summer. . . . Mr. Clark had trouble last season with the ice containing foreign matter [chaff], but he guarantees there will not be any cause for complaint this year." Clark harvested ice from two ponds in East Fairhaven—a four-acre pond on Mill Road, and a one-acre pond on Washington Street—with icehouses at both sites. Once harvested, the large ice slabs (usually four feet by four feet by the thickness of the ice) stayed cold in the small houses through the primitive insulation method of covering them with mounds of hay. In the summer of 1912, Clark's ice ranged in thickness from nine to 12 inches.

COTTAGE GIFT SHOP - FAIRHAVEN, MASS.

The Cottage Gift Shop was located on Huttleston Avenue near the Fairhaven Drive-In Theater. It was operated by Dorothy Cardinal from the late 1940s into the early 1950s. Today, a hot dog restaurant occupies the building.

This panoramic view showing Westdale Pharmacy on Sconticut Neck Road was created by combining two separate postcards made by a local photography buff in the 1940s. Westdale Pharmacy was established by Mr. and Mrs. Everett Daley. Local residents will notice that most of the buildings in this view are still standing. Westdale's was later bought by Robert E. Browne and added to his chain of Browne's pharmacies.

"Cape-Way Cafe"
Route U. S. 6, Fairhaven, Mass.
George Sirois, Owner

Friendly service and home-cooked food could be found at the Cape Way in East Fairhaven, located just a few feet from the Mattapoisett town line. While urban sprawl, with supermarkets, shopping plazas, housing developments, service stations and car lots have encroached upon East Fairhaven's once rural landscape, the Cape Way Cafe is still serving draft beer and pickled eggs. For many years, the Cape Way was well known as the last call in Fairhaven—the only bar still serving drinks at 1:00AM.

Long before the Interstate highway, U.S. Route 6 was the only thoroughfare to Cape Cod from points west, making Fairhaven a welcome stop for travelers. The Skipper Restaurant was located on Route 6 at the Fairhaven end of the bridge from New Bedford. With docking space available, it was once considered as a permanent site for the whaleship **Charles W. Morgan.**

Since the development of Route 6 in the early 1930s, many roadside motels have come and gone. The Havenwood Motor Court, established in 1930 and located in East Fairhaven, withstood the onslaught of highway development until 2002, when it was bought and razed to make room for a pizza franchise.

HAVENWOOD MOTOR COURT, Fairhaven, Mass.
ALICE CAMERON DeCOFFEE, Proprietor

This postcard of the interior of Browne's Pharmacy was sent to announce the celebration of the pharmacy's fifth year in business (1915). Browne's, at the corner of Main and Centre streets, was one of six in a chain of pharmacies begun by Frederick T. Browne, Sr., of Dartmouth, and located throughout the region. This pharmacy was popular for its ice cream parlor atmosphere, soda fountain, and confectionery. Among the items for sale at Browne's were Jamaicol cough medicine, corn shellers (to remove corns), Irish Moss Cultibalm (hand lotion), Browne's celebrated fruit punch, and Necco irregular chocolates at $.29/lb.

Browne's was located in the former Second Church of Christ building, which was built in 1794. In 1853, the church was raised one story, turned and renamed the Phoenix Block. The second floor, known as Phoenix Hall, was used for town meetings, plays, dances, suppers, caucuses and graduations. The cannon out front was the one first mounted by Nathaniel Pope in anticipation of a British attack in 1778. It now resides at Fort Phoenix.

PHOENIX HALL, FAIRHAVEN

H. S. HUTCHINSON & CO.   NEW BEDFORD, MASS.

AT FAIRHAVEN BRIDGE

Trains & Trolleys

Motorman James E. Card and Conductor Charles Bosworth pose before their trusty car at Oxford Heights in 1907. The Oxford line first opened in 1873 and was one of the street railway's oldest. The original run was from downtown New Bedford to Riverside Cemetery. In 1907, the run was extended to Coggeshall Street.

This postcard is a rare view of the short-lived experiment called the "trackless trolley," tried out on Sconticut Neck Road in late 1914. Wires were strung for a mile or so down the neck for the sleek bus with its steel-rimmed tires and hard-rubber-treads. The operation lasted only through the autumn because of mechanical problems and power shortages. Also, because service began late in the season, ridership was poor.

94

Widening Main Street, circa 1900. With the success of the street railway system and the advent of the automobile, the main streets in town were in need of alteration.

The depot of the Fairhaven Branch of the Old Colony Railroad, built in 1859 as a one-story brick building with a slate roof, accommodated two tracks. Primarily used for freight, the railroad performed to mixed reviews. When a shipment of goods to Boston was delayed for unknown reasons in 1870, officials were notified: "...waited three days for goods to ship west. We advise you send goods by oxen team in the future: quicker if not cheaper." The depot was demolished in 1929 and passenger service officially ended.

Street View Fairhaven Mass.

The Hurricane of 1938

On September 21, 1938, New England was rocked by the most insidious storm ever recorded—a killer force that took nearly 700 lives. Winds of 186 mph and 40-foot waves pounded Fairhaven, tossing the fishing fleet like toy boats in a bathtub, and littering the wharves with splintered debris. The scene above looks down Peirce and Kilburn Wharf from Fort Street on the morning after.

Long stretches of homes along the beaches, such as these cottages on Sconticut Neck, were pummeled. Flood tides also struck inland damaging homes, businesses and factories. Raging winds tore off roofs and ripped down walls. Fishing boats, yachts, and even freighters were swept onto the streets by flooding waters.

Fairhaven Mass.

Owners survey the destruction at Hathaway Braley Wharf. Compounding the severity of the winds, the storm hit Buzzards Bay at high tide and at the autumnal equinox—the highest tide of the year—causing a "storm surge" or tidal wave. Fairhaven suffered five fatalities, including Palmer's Island lighthouse keeper Mabel Small, who died when the boathouse she was in collapsed and the sea washed her away.

A view of the shore from the bridge near Pope's Island. This photograph was taken from the vicinity of the New Bedford Yacht Club, which was completely leveled and washed away. In 1938, the communications network for alerting residents of hurricanes was still rudimentary. Because roads, rails, and telegraph and telephone lines were washed out, urgent messages from New York to eastern New England were sent to Cape Cod via London and Paris.

Beach and Wigwam Beach
Sconticut Nk.

Summer Colonies

Long before English settlers arrived in Fairhaven, the Wampanoag people were coming to her shores in the summer to fish. This area was called "Sconticut," meaning "a fair place to live." Today, the peninsula that extends south into Buzzards Bay, called Sconticut Neck, is home to hundreds of summer and year-round residents. Over the years, many small, seasonal hamlets, or "colonies," have been established along the craggy coast. Most of the cottages in them are modest dwellings rented or owned by working families from industrial cities like New Bedford, Fall River and Brockton. While Cape Cod may have a wider profile and command a higher price, Sconticut Neck has been a paradise for the local populace. This last selection of postcards celebrates Fairhaven's most unique gift of nature—the New England coast.

STORE AT WILBUR POINT, SCONTICUT NECK, FAIRHAVEN, MASS.

Wilbur Point

Wilbur Point is the southern tip of Sconticut Neck. Once a 90-acre farm owned by the Delano Family, it was sold to Edwin Wilbur in 1877, who came up with the idea to rent summer cottages. His son, Horatio "Nelson" Wilbur, popularized Edwin's dream. In 1898, Nelson built four cottages that he rented as a summer retreat for hunters, vacationers and game players. In a few short years, his summer colony expanded to 16 cottages and included bath houses, a bowling alley, billiard room, grocery store (above), scallop shed, icehouse, carriage house, and boathouse. The postcards in this set date between 1910 and 1915. In the scene below, Edwin Wilbur entertains a young summer guest.

SHORE SCENE, WILBUR POINT, SCONTICUT NECK, FAIRHAVEN, MASS.

Greetings from Wilbur Point, Sconticut Neck, Fairhaven, Mass.

The Wilbur Point colony was self-sustaining with few amenities other than well water. Yet its cottages were an immediate success, rented by families wanting to escape life in the bustling industrial world. Families arrived at the train station in New Bedford or Mattapoisett and were met by Mr. Wilbur. He loaded their trunks into his wagon and brought them to the Point. This card shows the carriage house, which was shared by guests.

Here, a less inviting winter scene shows the stark, imposing natural beauty of the rocky beach.

WOULDN'T A SUMMER COTTAGE BE COOL AT WILBUR POINT, FAIRHAVEN, MASS.?

Why have we not heard from you? Have been expecting to hear for a long time. Katherine was here and spent one night while in Fairhaven. I did not see Parker at all. E. called on the vessel. This is Sam in the boat in the picture. Let us hear from you. Come when you can

Dora.

View of Wilbur Point, Sconticut Neck, Fairhaven, Mass.

Nelson Wilbur's guests were often repeat customers, and if we're to believe the claim written on this card, one such repeat guest has apparently found her way into the picture. Nelson himself spent much of his 93 years at the point. He died in 1965. Old-timers still remember him in his old truck, delivering milk from his cows and ice from his ice pond to the 16 cottages, or in his boat laden with vegetables passing under the bridge and up the river to his winter home in Acushnet, or driving his dump car filled with lobsters to the market in New Bedford.

While the brave swim in the warm but rocky waters of Buzzards Bay, other folks hunt for small crabs beneath stones on the beach. Barely visible on the horizon are several of the nine Elizabeth Islands.

BATHING AT WILBUR POINT, SCONTICUT NECK, FAIRHAVEN, MASS.

Greetings from Wilbur Point, Sconticut Neck, Fairhaven, Mass.

A glacial garden of rock and ledge, Wilbur Point was farmed by the Delano family from the late 1700s into the mid-1800s.

The two views of Wilbur Point below, are taken from Angelica Island, just off the point's southwestern tip.

Because the area had always been an important farming, hunting and shellfishing area for the Wampanoag, the Delanos, after expropriation, allowed the Indians to farm the rocky island they called Angelico or Angelica.

Greetings from Wilbur Point, Sconticut Neck, Fairhaven, Mass.

VIEW OF WILBUR POINT, SCONTICUT NECK, FAIRHAVEN, MASS.

103

NORTH END WIGWAM BEACH, FAIRHAVEN, MASS.
Cottages to let.   Apply to R. T. REFUSE, 45 Richmond St., New Bedford, Mass.

Wigwam Beach

Robert T. Refuse, an immigrant from Nova Scotia, came to Wareham in 1873 and worked as a blacksmith. Later, he moved to New Bedford and worked in maintenance on horsecars for the street railway company; then bought a blacksmith shop on Acushnet Avenue. In 1899, Refuse sold his business and bought the Hathaway farm on Sconticut Neck. Here he built a summer colony and named it Wigwam Beach.

Wigwam Beach is on the east, or leeward, side of Sconticut Neck, facing Naskatucket Bay. With tranquil waters, rich in shellfish, the area has been as pleasing and nourishing to the vacationers as it was to the Wampanoag. The cluster of houses on the beach borders a sacred Indian burial ground.

Cottages & Water front
Wigwam Beach, Sconticut Nk.

Priscilla, Wigwam Beach, Fairhaven, Mass

Only one small shack stood on the land that Robert Refuse purchased. Remodeled and enlarged, it became known as "The Wigwam." Mr. Refuse built additional cottages, continuing to give them Indian names—presumably out of respect for the ancient burial ground that occupied his land. To dignify the cemetery he cleaned up the oak scrub around the gravestones and planted trees to create shade. Though there are no names on the gravestones, according to Jabez Delano's notes they are the graves of the Simon family—reportedly the last pure Wampanoag family in North America.

Mr. Refuse, like Mr. Wilbur at Wilbur Point, cleverly merchandised his summer colony by creating a set of postcards that showcased and promoted the cottages through the unwitting efforts of his tenants.

Ramona, Wigwam Beach, Fairhaven, Mass.

Spent 7th + 8th of Aug. and the week of the 14th. Swell time. Our cottage.

Ice House at Wigwam Beach, Fairhaven, Mass.

WAHONOMIN COTTAGE, WIGWAM BEACH, FAIRHAVEN, MASS.

Cottages rented by the month or season.
Address R. T. Refuse, New Bedford, Mass.

Hiawatha, Wigwam Beach, Fairhaven, Mass.

Grocery Store, Wigwam Beach, Fairhaven, Mass.

Erected around 1910, the summer colony at Wigwam Beach consisted of about 15 cottages and included a grocery store, icehouse, and a boathouse supplied with canoes and rowboats. For the first three decades, cottages were rented, usually for two to four weeks at a time, often by the same families every year. Eventually, the cottages were sold to folks who made them their own summer homes, and most of them still stand today.

Nokomis, Wigwam Beach, Fairhaven, Mass.

Sagwa, Wigwam Beach, Fairhaven, Mass.

Powwow, Wigwam Beach, Fairhaven, Mass.

Most of Mr. Refuse's Wigwam tenants were, like himself, from first-generation immigrant working-class families. They became well acquainted with one another, and many were from the same city parishes. When the Refuse family began selling off the cottages in the late 1920s, most were bought by the summer tenants. Today, descendants of these families still own them.

Bathing at Wigwam Beach, Fairhaven, Mass.

OWAISSA COTTAGE, WIGWAM BEACH, FAIRHAVEN, MASS.

Cottages rented by the month or season.
Address R. T. Refuse, New Bedford, Mass

107

Overlooking a large marsh called the "moorlands" were rooms available to let at Camp Knollmere on Knollmere beach. At this unlucky hamlet on the east side of Shaw's Cove in East Fairhaven, all but two of about 15 houses were destroyed by the Hurricane of 1938. In her note written on the back of this postcard sent in 1921, Miss K. writes, "This is an ideal place for fishing and blueberrying."

Summer residents never went hungry at Red Rock Beach. The menu at Worley's Pavilion featured the latest in 1950s fast-food cuisine. Following the hurricanes in 1938, 1944 and 1954, people of Sconticut Neck wasted little time in rebuilding their beachfront communities. Worley's Pavilion, built around 1956, was situated dangerously close to the high tide mark, yet, it survived the hurricane in 1960. It was destroyed by fire in 1964.

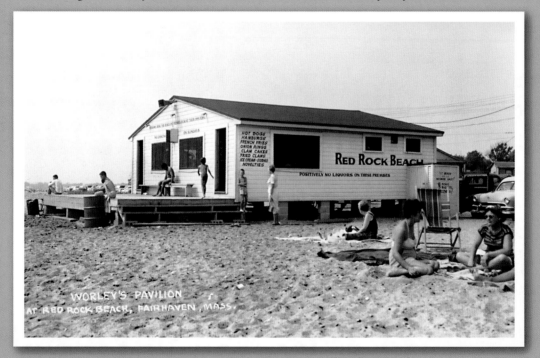

Year-round shanties and summer cottages share the beach at Harbor View on Fairhaven's south shore, east of Fort Phoenix, circa 1930s. Most of these houses were wiped out by the Hurricane of 1938.

Low tide reveals one of Sconticut Neck's sandiest shores—the north section of Pope Beach, circa 1930. None of these houses survived the Hurricane of 1938.

West Island

To the east of the southern tip of Sconticut Neck lies the island called Nakata by the Wampanoag and West Island by the English—for Stephen West, son-in-law of John Cooke, Mayflower passenger and one of Fairhaven's first landowners. The island seems at one time to have been the property of King Philip. A deed recorded in Plymouth signed "P the mark of Philip the Sachem," conveyed it for 10 pounds sterling "with liberty to make yards upon for pasturing of cattle and also for free range for cattle in winter, but to take them away about planting time." The deed between Philip and John Cooke contained a provision that, should a whale find its way onto the shore, it was to be divided equally between the two.

TOWER - West Island
Sconticut NK

Until the mid-1940s, with the exception of a small section owned by the U.S. government (where a concrete watchtower constructed during World War II still stands), there was only one house on the island— the 150-year-old home of Captain John T. Besse and his family. Once used as a grazing ground for cattle, West Island was also a hunting ground for deer, geese and duck. Mrs. Eldred Besse, whose husband descended from Captain Besse, remembers having to row out to meet her relatives. "It was a million miles away from anywhere," she recalls. Captain Besse and his wife raised their family in this remote area, where fishing and hunting were as important a livelihood as farming. "It was quite a sight to watch the cows swimming across the island for summer grazing," says Mrs. Besse.

The causeway bridge connecting Long Island (in background) with West Island has long been a favorite spot for young divers and "snapper-blue" (young bluefish) fishermen.

West Island Scene, Buzzards Bay, Mass.

110

This view from West Island's western shore shows the causeway with Wilbur Point in the distant background. The boats may belong to local shellfishermen, as these shallow waters are ripe with clams and quahogs.

Pleasure craft, vintage 1950s, are safe at Earl's Marina in the protected cove on the lee side of Long Island.

West Island
Fairhaven Estates, Fairhaven, Mass.

Aerial views of West Island on these and following pages were taken around 1950 to promote development of Fairhaven Estates. The view above was made as the plane passed over Wilbur Point. West Island's size has been given in various accounts as between 650 and 1000 acres, depending on the tide.

With the exception of the land owned by the government, the island was purchased by Arthur F. Gobron of Watertown in 1946 for $50,000. Gobron immediately began to create Fairhaven Estates, a $1 million project that parceled 2000 small lots with at least 1200 cottages. Lots were to be sold for $300 to $500, with advertising directed at the surrounding area. Every prospective homeowner would be interviewed by the company. "There will be no tarpaper shacks and no houses costing less than $1200," said Gobron. (**Standard-Times**, 3/13/46)

West Island
Fairhaven Estates, Fairhaven, Mass.

This view shows the quasi-developed condition of the struggling new development. By 1950, only 150 houses had been built, most of them seasonal. By 1963, 400 cottages had been built, 100 of which were year-round. Though Fairhaven Estates carved out a large chunk of the island's densely wooded brush, it left a large area that would later be designated as a wildlife preserve.

Although the Estates project was never completed as planned, the land was eventually developed by private concerns. In the distance are the south shores and peninsulas of Mattapoisett, Marion and Wareham.

West Island
Fairhaven Estates, Fairhaven, Mass.

West Island is located east of the southern tip of Sconticut Neck. In this view, circa 1950, the causeway bridge leads from Sconticut Neck (top), passes through Long Island, and makes a sandy entrance into the newly built Fairhaven Estates. The distance from Sconticut Neck to Long Island is about 450 feet, and about 700 feet between Long Island and West Island.

Index

Bibliography

Adams, Oscar Fay. "A New England Architect and His Work." *New England Magazine*, June 1907.

_____. *A Wind to Shake the World: The Story of the 1938 Hurricane*. Boston: Little Brown, 1976.

Bernard, Donald R. *Tower of Strength: A History of Fort Phoenix*. Fairhaven, 1975.

Boss, Judith A., and Joseph D. Thomas. *New Bedford: A Pictorial History*. Norfolk: Donning Co., 1983.

Crapo, Henry Howland. *The New Bedford Directory*. New-Bedford: Charles Taber, 1859.

Cummings, O. R. *Transportation Bulletin No. 85 – Union Street Railway*. Warehouse Point, Connecticut: National Railway Historical Society, 1980.

Dias, Earl J. *Henry Huttleston Rogers: Portrait of a Capitalist*. Fairhaven: Millicent Library, 1974.

Ellis, Leonard Bolles. *History of New Bedford and Its Vicinity, 1620-1892*. Syracuse: D. Mason & Co., 1892.

Federal Writers' Project. *Fairhaven, Massachusetts, American Guide Series*. Fairhaven, 1939.

Gifford, Pardon B., and Zephaniah W. Pease. *100th Anniversary of the New Bedford Mercury, 1807–1907*. New Bedford: Mercury Publishing Co., 1907.

Gillingham, James L. and others. *Brief History of the Town of Fairhaven, Massachusetts; Prepared in Connection with the Celebration of Old Home Week, July 26-31, 1903*. New Bedford: Standard Printing, 1903.

Harris, Charles Augustus. *Old-Time Fairhaven*. 2 vols. New Bedford: Reynolds Printing, 1947.

Hubbard, Elbert. *Little Journeys to the Homes of Great Businessmen*. East Aurora, New York: The Roycrofters, 1909.

Hurricane: 1944. New Bedford: The Standard-Times, 1944.

Hurricane: 1954! New Bedford: The Standard-Times, 1954.

Hurricane: …New England's Stricken Area, September 21, 1938. Waltham: Waltham News-Tribune, 1938.

Hutchinson, H. S. & Co. *New Bedford and Fairhaven, Massachusetts*. New Bedford: H. S. Hutchinson, 1903.

Knipe, Mabel Hoyle. *Century of Concern: …Improvement Association, 1883-1983*. Fairhaven: Millicent Library, 1983.

_____. *Czar of Fairhaven: A Portrait of John I. Bryant*. Fairhaven: Millicent Library, 1980.

_____. *The First Gift: The Story of Rogers Grammar School*. Fairhaven: Millicent Library, 1977.

_____. *House of Transition*. Fairhaven: Millicent Library, 1977.

_____. *"Thee Will Fill It Up!" The Story of Robert Cushman Park*. Fairhaven: Millicent Library, 1979.

Millicent Library. *Dedicatory Exercises, Millicent Library, January 30, 1893*. New Bedford, 1893.

New Topographical Atlas of Surveys, Bristol County Massachusetts. Philadelphia: Everts & Richards, 1895.

Pease, Zephaniah W. *History of New Bedford*. New York: Lewis Historical Pub. Co., 1918.

_____. "New Bedford, Massachusetts: Its History, Industries, Institutions and Attractions." New Bedford: New Bedford Board of Trade and Mercury Publishing Company, 1889.

Potter, Mabel L. "History of Sconticut Neck." Unpublished, 1945. Millicent Library collection, Fairhaven.

Radcliffe, Helen Hiller. "History of Wilbur Point." Unpublished, 1980. Millicent Library collection, Fairhaven.

Ricketson, Daniel. *The History of New Bedford, Bristol County, Massachusetts: Including a History of the Old Township of Dartmouth…from Their Settlement to the Present Time*. New Bedford: The Author, 1858.

Rodman, Samuel, and Zephaniah W. Pease. *The Diary of Samuel Rodman: A New Bedford Chronicle of Thirty-Seven Years, 1821-1859*. New Bedford: Reynolds Printing Co., 1927.

Rodgers, Patricia H. *Three for a Nickel: Martha's Vineyard Postcards, 1900–1925*. Cambridge: Aqua Press, 2002

Pupils of Fairhaven High School. *About Our High School*. 2 ed. Fairhaven: Millicent Library, 1954. Reprint, 1979.

Spinner Publications. *A Picture History of Fairhaven*. New Bedford: Spinner Publications, 1986.

Thomas, Joseph D. "Pioneers of the Banks." In *Spinner…, Volume III*. New Bedford: Spinner Publications, 1984.

Tripp, Thomas. "The Story of Fairhaven." Unpublished, 1929. Millicent Library collection, Fairhaven.

Trolleygrams. New Bedford: Union Street Railway Company, 1922–1928.

Twain, Mark, and Millicent Library. *Mark Twain and Fairhaven*. 2d. ed. Fairhaven: Millicent Library, 1926.

Whitman, Nicholas. *A Window Back: Photography in a Whaling Port*. New Bedford: Spinner Publications, 1994.

Worth, Henry B. "Oxford Village, Fairhaven." In *Old Dartmouth Historical Sketches*. New Bedford: Old Dartmouth Historical Society, 1915.

Newspaper Articles

"A Fairhaven Inn." *Standard-Times* April 17,1983.

"A Stupendous Scheme." *Evening Standard* October 3, 1902.

"Appeals Board Grants Owner Right to Repair." *Fairhaven Star* April 26, 1934.

"Announcement at Peirce and Kilburn." *Fairhaven Star* November 14, 1930.

Clark, Richard T. "The Good Shepherd of Fairhaven." *Boston Herald*, May 14, 1971.

"Grimshaw Clambake House." *The Standard-Times* September 6, 1964.

"Housing Project Planned on Isle." *The Standard-Times*, March 13, 1946.

"Improvement Association Bath Houses." *Fairhaven Star* April 29, 1905.

Kirschbaum, William G. "Popular Fort Phenix." *The Evening Standard* July 14, 1900.

"Landmark Burns." *The Standard-Times* August 13, 1967.

"Local Men Buy Boat Yard Here." *Fairhaven Star* January 19, 1956.

Mitchell, Marian. "Wrecking Bar Again at Work on…Rogers." *Sunday Standard-Times* August 31, 1941.

"Nearly All From 10 to 12 Inches Thick and Clear." *Fairhaven Star* April 8, 1912.

"New Bath Houses Were Open Today." *Fairhaven Star* July 8, 1916.

"New Bedford Man Likes Air Photography.…" *The New Bedford Sunday Standard*, September 5, 1926.

"Obituary: Alonzo G. Van Nostrand." *Fairhaven Star* November 9, 1923.

"Obituary: Robert T. Refuse." *Fairhaven Star* March 17, 1923.

"Orange Hued Bathing Suit Scares Away the Sharks." *Fairhaven Star* July 22, 1916.

"Photo Pioneer H. M. Wood Dies." *The Standard-Times*, September 23, 1950.

"Present and Past of Union Wharf." *Fairhaven Star* September 19, 1935.

"Rebuilt Dragger Launched Here." *Fairhaven Star* 1960.

Richard, Lori. "Revisiting the Old General Stores." *The Navigator* July 2002.

"Rudy Vallee Dines on Chicken Here." *Fairhaven Star* September 1, 1932.

"School Boys Building Muscles and Appetites." *Fairhaven Star* January 29, 1907.

"State Acquires Fort Phoenix Land." *Fairhaven Star* June 16, 1960

Stewardson, Jack. "With Pilot's Death an Island Loses Its Wings." *The Standard-Times* February 13, 1987.

"The Rogers School." *Morning Mercury* September 4, 1885.

"Town Planners Refuse to Endorse Petition." *Fairhaven Star* March 22, 1934.

"Unitarian Memorial Church Parish House." *Fairhaven Star* August 1, 1903.

"Wharf Once Owned by Kin of President Sold Here." *The Standard Times* March 11, 1937.

"Where Sleep the Mighty Sconticut Tribe." *Fairhaven Star* July 30, 1934.

Spinner Publications, Inc. · New Bedford, Massachusetts
For information about Spinner books, calendars and historic photographs,
visit www.spinnerpub.com or call 800-292-6062